Top Dinosaurs

Maoliosa Kelly
Jon Hughes   Ali Teo

Contents

Dinosaurs   2
Tyrannosaurus rex   4
Brachiosaurus   6
Compsognathus   8
Velociraptor   10
Stegosaurus   12
Top dinosaurs   14

Collins

Dinosaurs lived on Earth millions of years ago.

There were many different dinosaurs. Here are some of them.

Velociraptor

Compsognathus

Tyrannosaurus rex
(tie-ran-o-sor-us rex)

These dinosaurs were very scary. They had long, sharp teeth.

They had short arms but no-one knows why.

Brachiosaurus
(brack-i-o-sor-us)

These dinosaurs were very tall. They were as tall as houses.

They were as heavy as 15 elephants.

Compsognathus
(comp-sog-nay-thus)

These dinosaurs were very small.
They were as small as hens.

They were as heavy as cats.

Velociraptor
(vell-oss-ee-rap-tor)

These dinosaurs were very fast.
They could run as fast as cars.

They had big, sharp claws.

Stegosaurus
(steg-o-sor-us)

These dinosaurs were very strong. They had plates on their backs and spikes on their tails.

They had very small brains. Their brains were as small as walnuts.

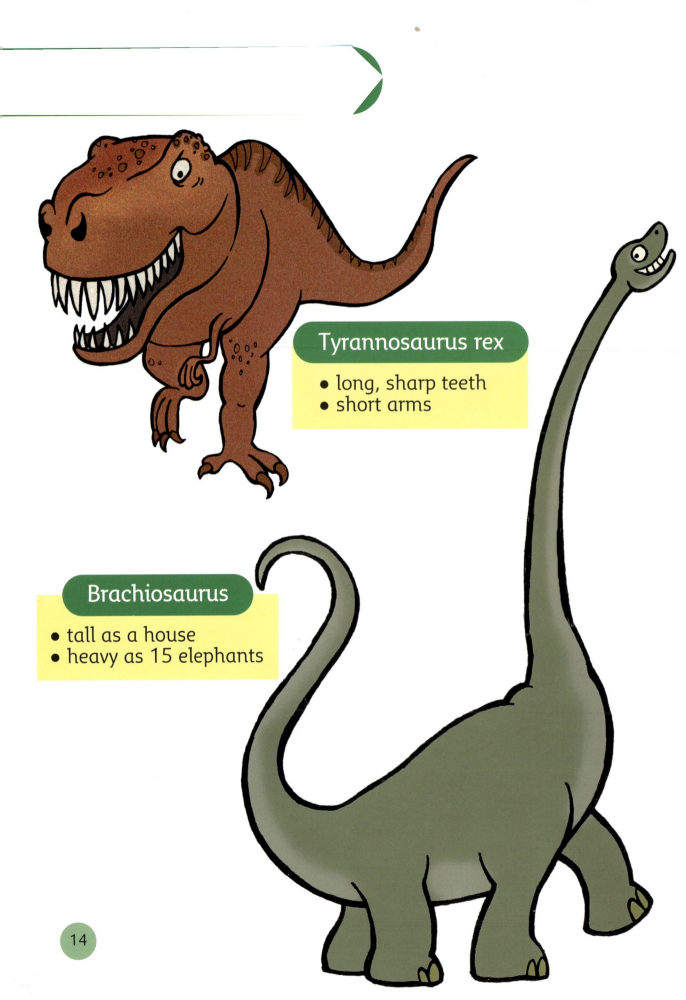

Velociraptor
- fast as a car
- big, sharp claws

Compsognathus
- small as a hen
- heavy as a cat

Stegosaurus
- very strong
- very small brain

Ideas for reading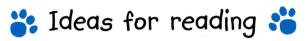

Written by Linda Pagett B.Ed (hons), M.Ed
Lecturer and Educational Consultant

Learning objectives: Using the terms fiction and non-fiction and understanding their different features; predicting text, reading on leaving a gap and re-reading; reading words with initial consonant clusters; taking turns to speak and listen.

Curriculum links: Numeracy: Shapes, Space and Measure

High frequency words: were, lived, on, was, very, had, as, they

Interest words: Tyrannosaurus Rex, Brachiosaurus, Compsognathus, Velociraptor, Stegosaurus

Word count: 174

Resources: small wipe boards and pens

Getting started

- Read the title and discuss what the children already know about dinosaurs.
- Walk through the text with the children and talk about what kind of book it is and what features they can spot (e.g. contents, index). Can any of the children identify the dinosaurs? Point out the strange dinosaur words and read them to the children.
- Ask what the proper word is for books that tell us facts. Use the words *fiction* and *non-fiction*.
- Ask the children what to do if you get stuck on a word. Model how to read a sentence and leave a gap for a more difficult word, then go back and see what word 'fits'.

Reading and responding

- Ask the children to read independently and aloud – they may attempt to read the dinosaur words, but if they aren't sure ask them to move straight on to the right-hand pages.
- Praise children who predict unfamiliar words by leaving a gap and then finding a word that fits.
- Discuss pp14–15 together. What did they find out about dinosaurs? What kind of illustrations are they? How do we know what dinosaurs looked like?